It's Alive!

by Linda Yoshizawa

PEARSON

Scott Foresman

Editorial Offices: Glenview, Illinois • Parsippany, New Jersey • New York, New York
Sales Offices: Needham, Massachusetts • Duluth, Georgia • Glenview, Illinois
Coppell, Texas • Ontario, California • Mesa, Arizona

So Many Plants

There are all kinds of plants. Some are big, and some are small. Some grow tall on strong stems. Some are vines that climb up walls and fences. Some plants have fruit. Some have smooth stems and leaves. Some have hard, bumpy bark.

Some redwood trees grow to be 350 feet tall. That's taller than the Statue of Liberty.

3

All plants are different, but they are alike in some ways too. Big or small, they are all living things. They grow and they change. Some large plants start out as tiny seeds. When they get what they need, they grow into large plants.

Corn kernels are seeds that grow into tall stalks.

Plants grow almost everywhere. You can find plants in warm and cold climates. They can grow wherever they get the things they need. Plants need water, light, and air to live.

Crocus in the snow

Plants Need Water

Water dissolves nutrients from the soil so plants can use them. Nutrients are what living things need to grow and have energy.

The stem of a plant is filled with tiny tubes. The tubes carry water from the roots to the leaves. The leaves use the nutrients in the water to make food.

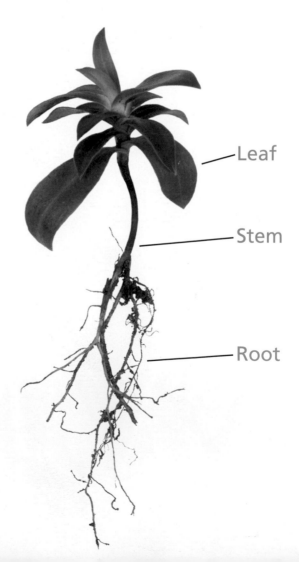

Leaf

Stem

Root

Even plants that grow in dry desert climates need water. Deserts do not get much rain. Desert plants have adapted to dry climates. For example, a cactus can store water in its stem. A cactus can live for a long time on a little bit of water.

Cactus

Plants Need Light

Plants need more than nutrients and water to grow. They also need light. Plants use the sunlight that falls on their leaves to make food.

This daisy gets a lot of light. It is healthy.

Some plants need a lot of light. Some only need a little. If plants cannot get the light they need, they will not be healthy. They may even die.

This daisy got very little light. It died.

Plants Need Air

Plants need water and sunlight to survive. They need one more thing too. Like all living things, plants need air.

Air is made up of many different gases. One of those gases is carbon dioxide. Plants take carbon dioxide from the air. Along with water, nutrients, and light, they use it to make food.

Plants and animals share the air around them. They use air in different ways.

Animals breathe in oxygen. They breathe out carbon dioxide. Plants take in carbon dioxide and give off oxygen. In this way, they both need each other.

Plants help keep the air clean for people and animals.

When plants get what they need, they grow healthy and strong. When plants are healthy and strong, our environment is a better place.

We know plants are at work when we harvest apples from a tree or grapes from a vine. We also know plants are at work when we breathe fresh, clean air.

Fruit and flowers may grow on trees, bushes, or vines.